Poetry for Mr Gould

Joel Schueler

Acknowledgements

A Night Off Course, **Pennsylvania Literary Journal**, August 2017

Yours Finely, **The Dawntreader**, October 2017

I've Seen You About, **The Brasilia Review**, November 2017

Music makes, **FIVE:2:One**, August 2018

Some golf club in Highworth, **Why Vandalism?**, August 2019

Send the bailiffs in, **The Pangolin Review**, November 2019

Unstill, **Jeanette Cheezum's calvalcadeofstars**, January 2020, (Republished) in **SOUL Literary Magazine** August 2020

I understand why you died tonight, **Poetry Festival**, May 2020, (Republished) in **WILDsound Festival Review** May 2020

The Unwashed Monologue, **BlogNostics**, July 2020, (Republished) in **Sparks of Calliope**, September 2020

Shell(ey), **bluepepper**, July 2020

Memoranda, **Lyrical Passion Poetry E-Zine**, July 2020

Screened Secrets, **The Blotter Magazine**, August 2020

Church of St. Michael's, **Better than Starbucks**, September 2020

A Certain Virus, **whimperbang**, September 2020

(Untitled), **Shot Glass Journal**, October 2020

Glass for the Looking, **Cacti Fur**, October 2020

Imaginings of the Familial, **London Poetry Magazine**, December 2020

<u>Questions of Validation</u>, **The Brown Envelope Book (Anthology)**, April 2021

Land, **Wild Things Zine**, April 2021

all else ego forgot, **EgoPHobia**, June 2021

Water Aid, **The Templeman Review,** July 2021

Debauchery Diaries, **Raven Cage Zine,** July 2021

Contents

The Room of Every Day

I

This is the abnormal room of every day.
The dead legs of the computer desk
and the coffee table, one each,
have been moulded
back to rightful positions sometime after
derailments of mind. There rests a knowing
in the flare-ups. The finally arrived
beige bin sacks are in a huddle near the TV
as if to keep warm from the oncoming autumn.
Days pass in varieties of oneness.
    It is a suitable place for a ruminant
during the week; not so
on weekends, when collisions between alcohol and humans
spark sounds of inharmony in the empty outside.
Uncarpeted, the linoleum is of a sick green. It bears
the brunt of footsteps but for some matting
purchased just after moving. By the settee, ghastily greyed
but relatively clean, a ridged runner in a jumble
of creases is a stampede in a still frame.
There is a TV box that looks electrifyingly uninteresting.
Of technological prudery it roosts
chummily on a portable radiator
movable by wheels. The box overhangs from the radiator
for a precarious foothold as if a skateboard
is in its possession. The unremembered television set is in need
of a dust down. No doubt once up to snuff it is detained
like a fossil of the industrial scene. The rolled round

throw takes its place by the curtains at the middle
end of the room like some peach thunderhead. If it had limbs
it would be on all fours. The gaps between untidiness
ameliorate a settling in. The bulb in the shade plays
havoc with each portending shadow it casts. The shadows
are languorous and laid up in this place, in a choir of silence.

II

The world has turned
a new page today
in whose plans a banana is armed with an armful of kiwi
in a fairway-green plastic bowl at the north-east corner
of the top-heavy
look of the uptight coffee table.
At the south-east corner
lives Van Gogh. He is on a coaster,
and again, to the south-west.
Like the larger-brother-given gift
above the computer
screen, the south-east coaster
is of his starry night: playing the evening
wisp on a flute. The obvious choice, it is the easiest
of the artist's pictures to like, and yet I find
it hard to prefer others more.
It is the artful hour of 1:23 a.m. A synergic meeting
of pepper and salt is taking place at the central end
of the coffee table whose wonkiness lifts
the salt in for a kiss with the pepper, jealous
it has more in its pot. How easily it forgets the giant
thimble of table salt behind it, just waiting to finish.
Ikea and Wilco cut a look back at me at the back

middle left of the room. Topped by towels once drying
is the Ikea bookcase two seasons
ahead for winter. North-west on the coffee-table
is an off-duty remote control, suturing the wan wound
of assorted papers beneath it. The papered walls
of the lampshades shaped like UFOs are too light-happy
and inviting to stem from the other side
of the galaxy. The systemetisation of the four-box
storage unit from Wilco is a medium
cry from the general order of this place —
ransacked and purged. A browner shade
of grey, the curtains blench in the wind when
the window allows them space. Running through rings
of Saturn—the curtain pole in usual circumstances
supported at three points—spraddles, for where the central point
would be, no wall exists.

A nineteen-year-old guitar laps up the esteem at being
the highest placed object on a chair of rubble. The rubble is such
that one would do well to make out the rage
of colours, multifarious and deep, and the shilly-shally
of patterned masterpieces that adorn the throw
underneath. On a door handle, an aqua blue
towel is doing its best impression of a jellyfish. Pens
are scattered at reachable opportunities. On the sideline
old objects laze in boxes, hoping to never be
moved. All objects behind me are equally interesting.

Behind the enjoyment is survival though rarely a crucible.
Of the pandemic that remains, if I am to play
by lockdown rules, there is no way
of my leaving it for normalcy for any great length of time.
This is the normal room of every day.

Autopilot

I seek out theft of a tear at your window
Downsized head, face full of glass.
Gobsmacked it would crack lines
Shaping winter willows — glade on glaze.
The night watchers believed
To keep all holy
Are to be paid in gold
At my behest.
They curate earth's energies
As art from the deep to the troposphere.
Rat-a-tat-tats once pointed scare
Too readily amidst the thunderclouds.
The night watchers will help them out too.

We have each other
In chokeholds listening to Galaxie 500's version
Of George Harrison's 'Isn't It a Pity?'
Lovemaking has given in
Its notice. Done for
Before we've begun.
The loop de loops of our whirlwind now wingedbacked memories
die out.

All I own is a cumbersome autopilot journey of backtrack.

Questions of Validation

Aye yai yai the show trial is here,
dust marks for the forehead
from stabs at x the last digger made,
dust marks for the forehead
to remind them of my asthma.
Introspective and unselfsparing — my attempt

at normal, but do I want to seem normal?
What was the self I wished not to spare
that I have forgotten? I wonder
if there once were balustrades
the length of the courthouse to prop up

the powerful. I am ushered in by someone
delighted they could pronounce my surname.
How can I be gobsmacked by anything
to come when I have been kicked
off the sick borrowing mercy money for the year

of my unofficial illness. I wait
to see if I'm a faker,
to see whether I'll re-embark the aeroplane
for the desperate I was ejected from
to learn if I'll officially be mental again.

'Dear sponger,

No parachute will be necessary.
Move away from the funds

without as much as a day to prepare
for your nothingness.

We wish you good luck
and then some to those
choosing between homelessness and suicide.'

It is known who it is from.
Known too is the outcome

if I answered the questions
the way they wanted.
The judge was my doctor all along.

I understand why you died tonight

I understand why you died tonight
why the devil grew his tail
as your mind became frail,
why the sky mistook him for an angel.

Vienna and Bruges, and all that is smooth —
when toe meets foreshore;
dark chocolate, the Louvre.

Of nard and koi, and all that is joy —
sparkling streams of cygnets,
hard liquor, soft toys.

And now for the news.

Lead ties to shank
surfeit from the crapulous,
there are those who wait for the
summer to fall
there are those who act
when tablet mountain calls,

who torched the trellis
watched the wind make it crawl

it's hard when no-one knows
where no-one goes
behind your wall.

Hurry, Fore!

There is a copse back in Highworth whose bellies of bark bulge
out of their rings
A coal-clinker remembrance
And the pother it leaves

Swipe of metal carving nitrogen, oxygen, argon,
Slubber the drive for the men who wait

The flanks of those trunks
Evince not a gesture
Of an inner howl,
Dauntless and stout
Beneath their ostentation of crown and canopy

Occluded are felt visions of the immigrant white warhead
From eyelets in the rind
Reconstructed for anthropoidal delectation,
Their intellections for paganica
Greenly perspicacious like a callow lyrebird.
Another popped question, another *I do*
The living beringed aren't quite what they seem.

all else ego forgot

I place the bowl in front of me
to fill it with ego

the latter like cereal
is not nor could be,
no matter
empty as it seems.
I leave ego
ego leaves me
re-entering fullness.

Unstill

I am the water carrier
polisher of burdens,
singing strong hymns of candour
I am the cored child seeking brutal temperance.
Cursed against the hymns are men becoming clocks.
Their echoes frowning faces at crystal waters while I hear,
not ever, an album more
depressing
than *Berlin*, nor more crafted in its fatalist desolation, that
when they say it panned, I
smell it stealthily creep, disposing its ashes in the hearts of the sad;
ashes
frozen from a subject undead, and how
it had to be that way.
People of a normal world do not take such a sting,
watching the homeless and the lowly ration
malady.
Voices of parallel universes discordantly meet,
men swig the air hoping for city dirt
mellow jazz enter! The eerie, sickening voices, crawling out
tomorrow's megaphone of
death.
'Caroline Says II,' 'The Kids' and 'The Bed' all wash like a
threesome of colour dyed in melancholia.
The singer can barely get the words out he is so bored of life.
The subject splashes
amidst wild perfumes,
wailing whilst waltzing with druids by runic stones

her white sun
crashes
aside Alaska.

Church of St. Michael's

Hummingbird at St. Michael's where they bury the dead,
worn, of poor upkeep and cannot be read
names overrun with blotches of white
bell sound of eve in first July light.
Neatly, contrarily lives grass spooked by cuts
the groundskeeper made time long before dusk.

Hirsute green base with palm brushed through
crisp and flexible sounds ensue
flowers of a white alive like snow
watch the dwellers on young death row.

Ellipsis

What are memories but fragments of time
belonging to you and me
seldom written
in a clear hand
as mind-made notes,
or like book covers and postcards
said goodnight to
by dust
when claims of memory
are repurposed
for advantageous imagery.
Offerings of panegyrics
should be made
to the numerically minded
who are useful
to have on your team
at the pub quiz
particularly when there is a good prize
to be had.
How often we reshape
our memories into moments
of our lives
we'd have preferred were their source
that never turned up.

●

I slink away to Little Time
remembering how I remembered

events with the undeveloped mind
fine-tuning historicity —
my family but one on the inky waves
which smouldered and smudged
like birthmarks of night,
returning from the African continent
my dad's senses first
discovered as the world.

●

Piecing childhood flashbacks into fully grown memories is
mending a patchwork quilt.
\\\

●

In an over-intake of blues / bandage-white clouds / lust to die as
draperies.

Australian of Other

There is nothing
an outreach of glued compassion
within right soul to left
field can fail to assist

said the thoughts I wanted
to blurt from a disused channel
of brain before
I realised I was pedagogish

or at least I felt you,
they, might think it so
if not tell me, or the inverse
of such facts might be true

as you said not to worry
afire with swollen benevolence
cremating me when for you
I became the sorry male

that bled for greater outlook
that festered between escapes from
that look you give for
that man you want.

the black dog menace

and Dennis is in
    and out
of girls' bodies,
    infrequently a
yellow moss,
    a disturbed lichen,
with Dennis
    just another
name for another person

    and every place so humongous
when you are small —
    the seismic
wonder launching through your veins —
    now looks uninspiring
now looks little
    and lost,
your senses grown
    miniscule,
eyes smaller yet,
    pupils pins,
but it's okay
    you're just depressed;
this time
    this moment
this blackened alleyway
    that you scream down,
the summer
    equinox

will hit
    and there is no happy ending, there is
no sad ending
there just is

Shell(ey)

I have brought you this shell
from the molluskan mortuary. Listen to it.
Hearsay says you can hear might
of sea here. Take this chump — not
the hunter just the picker, and hear sin
fall in. My lament sits this one out
because I took out the going of the dark
and stored it in the hole of this white and orange grave.
The lived-in jacket in my hand: gold
in a quartz vein. Anyway, how's everything with
you?

Send the bailiffs in

Send the bailiffs in
I could use the conversation.

Do bailiffs like flowers?
Which ones are for the grave?

I will put them on the table
out before arrival

to be planted all they like
— I am —
growing up to feel like them

judging not the people whose home stores I gracefully examine;
gracefully me, the bailiff with the ballerina past life —

with dainty little steps(,) I examine.
When is closing time, and when will everyone concerned just
want to go

home?
Small talk was never my forte and the job is a job that is just a
job

all that is mine.
I long for the example

set by the tenant
with

no possessions,
no possession

over
herself

the day her work is done.

Screened Secrets

I watch you like a spy in a minibus,
a drifter through oval-windowed seacraft.

My brain has downloaded a shape of your memory
mountaineering in and amongst my inner workings

along burbling blood streams
from a bulletproof hard drive.

Walking the street brushing off fairy dust
uptown, you could be anyone

not this thing, this attempt at personhood.
What is it we incognito online agents

of the night have in common?
We spade up the avalanche aftermath

at the gates of self. Our vacuous attempts
at arranging all components of our machinery

to compute society leave us
preferring trees to people

starting new everythings over finishing up
just because it's easier,

disusing bookmarks that remind us of grief
scoffing down ice cream at eight in the morning

losing so much
we cannot feel

found.

Homes seem so safe
until time breaks
into these waiting rooms
for death.

I waited by the bike rack to catch a glimpse

I waited by the bike rack to catch a glimpse. I felt hesitation at the borderline over which of the two territories you would declare if you knew what I was up to. One of the lands was called Stalk, the other called Sweet. It is not wise for me to stay here in town. I'm more likely to get coronavirus with all these people coming and going less inclined to socially distance than they ever were before during the lockdown, particularly after Cummingsgate.

I walked up to the silver rooms and then to the unthinkable no man's land of in and amongst the dead shade on a hot summer's day. I hoped for doves spinning out of starlight ecstatic in their flight—that was how it was before when I saw you two days previous at the bike rack. And I saw you that same day again cycling towards Rodborough, and then again by the canal when I was not ready to do anything about it.

I wonder if it is possible to ask the police to show me CCTV footage of a few days ago so that I could see your snazzy trousers once again—instantly identifiable even with my poor eyesight. I just walked past the hospital but there are no beds for the lost of heart.

Goodness I like this Cotswold brick. It is so much better than Harrow brick. I will walk as I have walked, not least for your cause. I have a friend who once lived down Bowbridge Lane where the hospital is. A handy place to live if you are a hypochondriac like me—for the crack-ups and the cracked up, unlike beautiful brick.

Now I have stumbled upon the burial grounds. You can hear the rush of so many souls walking billions of miles between them in life now called to rest in a peak of silence—a silence but for the crows who have no respect. As I stand here I feel like I am interacting with more people than I ever have in lockdown. A loose petal rolls around on the ground in the light wind from a fall, and I wonder, if like many of these graves I too will end up here in a grave all my own by them.

Some golf club in Highworth

I have found a tree I quite like,
it is the closest I will get to having a girlfriend.
I used to like golf
but then I realised how sad it was.
Click! Clock! go the lunar balls
behind sun-
blent me. I
who usually live in
the corner of a cupboard.
Behind me drivel distant voices
of golfing parlance,
in front, unidentified creatures
vibrate in the heather;
a code just for them.
The former's clickclocking,
shared love of shit attire and talk
they call banter—some young'uns, bantz—
discomposes
my sprockets of creativity, my chain of production;
a golf ball is lodged
between the radial projections.
I wouldn't be
so angry
if I wasn't so lonely.
They are probably alright, the golfers
like my tree.
I lie,
I am at a new tree today,
better for sitting by

and better hidden
from the golfers,
who are not here
but they were yesterday;
the fuckers.

Yours Finely

All the flowers in the world alive today
should their army of beauty musically assemble
welter close to a tuning singularly yours.

Amalgam

It is hard to suitably report
the spaciousness of the sky
that becomes me, that I become
        above the fields past Victorian brick.
        The sun makes us feel like our backs
        are breaking from its power. So much rain
                from all the years gone by on the grass; the mud
                 wears the day in a gown o' green. Groats
                and our overcoats belong to the scarecrow

                        fleeing before dawn. There are honeybees
                        and tall pine trees but scarecrow has gone.
                        The dead for me is somewhere safe.
                No boys attack in the graveyard,
                I can be who I want.
                I will create my own definition of boy
to rise like a mountainside
from loose hope. The dead
are like pets, respectful,
                giving no backchat. It is dead
                easy to be dead. In this backbreaking
                heat, I am. Who decides I am
                        not? That sunny wild lady down the next
                        road? Is it her maker, my maker, no maker?
                        Can trust survive in any of the others?

I've Seen You About

I've seen you about
The way you lurk and sparkle
Back in ignominious style,
Your chest of drawers a couple of spies.
Charitably in your goo I dive
You know it not how drunk you were
You never did glitter in crazed sobriety,
That head that sped up to feast on me
And others in ripened sundew.
You cackle when I fall, gurgle my time, preach at dismembered
feet in your dungeon.
You are back and you know it
O you are *so* back.

You will dance with another at my face
You will take cover from memory

   Shrivel me in your urn,
    Your paint is so dry, cancerous, crackling

The drawers are awake
Open, open!
Never cease in peering out.

A Certain Virus

It feels up jut of sternum,
it sees ripe while we see red.
Who shall claim the sun for us? That is one thing
we cannot rely on
other humans for. Our days remain inopportune,
our brainpower hijacked by screens.
The snakehead fixates on that which is driven by an impulse.
How superb us idlers are scaffolded
by the things money has bought
as we approach the worst financial crisis
we have ever seen; from an unfair economic system we created,
we shall take our medicine: depression.

Mudstone Mind

Eye-catching as you are brittle
like a collocation of differently coloured shales,
why I placed you there I do not know
in the memory of something yet to happen.

To Be

which?
Rocking in a chair

being easily here, or a rocker firing forth
somersaulting with no time to breathe.
There's a shearing going on tonight

a stuck-up, mortifying shearing —
don't ask questions if you impale
your pauses too, too ready

for opportunism
oh forget it all already
out of joint with the feeling

noting effulgent comings and goings —
yes you know the sorts who relax
and radiate in equal measure

who tantalise without a try
to impose their structures on anyone
keeping on through the cutting.

Stapled tongues sweep air with words
that, in others' auricles, nest cushily
ready for their welcome.

Studied doing-it-agains
is all I can muster
not well

paining at the anxious hour
the future goldens.
The annual fuck-up is here

and yet, and yet, and still yet
I want no slice of cake
from the artists of peace

who do,
never try;
to desire to cease desire to be

Observance

I met you before the long-tailed tit
gave a wave;
if sounds are sweet
its cry was fudge
skipping like a p/Pollock in the air, a   here, a check there, a
                                    dive
little skip more.

I feel so selfish in my observance
hindered by structure
and probability, for the avian flight is not yet over —
over our heads then away from sight
owned as ours.

I don't know
female or male
who its parents were
where it pings to next.
Observation is a preoccupied game,
the bird observes its own path too.

Perhaps, resting, it thinks up
a myriad
of nonverbal communications
the anthropic miss.
Observation has a losel edge.
Impermanence just dust

Land

Come wattle the land
Greenest grass that you can
You shall hear now how I pine for naturalism

A sun-learned land
And hard-of-hearing sand
Hark, see there that growing flock of waves

O'er the mushroomscape
Those cumulations from magnetised moon.
I don't say it believing it

But by saying it, it gives me hope
That her land will be mine, not only, but mine, only not.
For the ones for whom I thirst

Thrive in the picnic-quiet
Of refrigerated lands. Obstreperous lands. The goose on the
outpost
Needn't keep watch when life is pillowed by creature comforts.

Oh you idyllic fuck
aestheticising moderne cornucopias for the timorous at heart.

Glass for the Looking

And daybreak lifts from the Pacific
Like tracing paper from a hairdryer
Low setting.
There is not any living object
Of this world that turns to you,
Your honeycomb tiles
In your desert/dessert—depends what day it is—citadel.
Marram grass like wind-bent strands
Of floss coloured olive gesticulate to a
High tide
Reacquainted with a rusting fringe,
Flames for eyelashes
Medium burn.
A dribbling of gulls across the skyline —
Gunned down from sight at sundown.

Kindling has evaded all eyes of this day
Eyelashes have entered
Begrimed brown,
Toes made unlovely
Like those on ends of foot-bound quondam souls.
Panache of catwalk like hollow death.
I saw it all
Or did I?
A seascape for threadbare eyes looking out
The window
Of neither
A glass of truth nor self-reflection.

Then what?

Water Aid

In the fire-
making symphonies of sunrise
watch the grasslands cower under the cover
of dew.

The Gist

Presented in
the shape of a tower
for the lost souls
of Grenfell

Can't think of anything

The day is a soup.

Another time lifts

Into my throat and

I am too desperate to claim anything

Beyond stillness.

I'm listening to Daniel Johnston.

I'm listening because I'm afraid

Of hope, and its lies

And the way

They told me

I could be better.

Instead I am developing somewhere

Between the chaotic

And the unlinked.

Do you think of love?

Is there any single disentanglement

More energising and hopeful?

Oval feels Octagonal

An inrush of coagulated dreams

Marks murkiness

Of mind, reaching this room.

Sun — it knives

Well-rounded

Full-bodied English clouds.

One January is another's

Downer.

I had a friend who once told me
a joke about the holocaust—half my
family were affected by such a
pothole over humanity. I was not
offended by the joke. I may have
thought it a little distasteful but I
had no part of my being that felt ill
will towards the teller; he was a
thoroughly decent bloke and a joke
is a joke.
    Too many find nothing else to do
in their lives than search out codes
for the safes of provocation and
victimhood. Like stills taken of
trees, they become almost alive. The

difference between the squeezer and
the ballooner of free speech is the
way the mind is kept.

All this politically correct
bullshit. Sometimes some media
play on outrage until character
outage.

I have oftentimes not been
distressed enough to finish this
poem. Take me away from the
gallantry of my wishful being!

The ultimate clickbait troll—how
many of those social media posts
are people stirring for reaction, for
exposure, for more followers, to
provoke the most evocative or
shocking post without as much as a
thought in the right place?

We settle down to read them,
passing over how we lucked out on
literacy.

What is happening to the climate
in the UK? Have our minds become
as dull as our weather? We used to
at least work towards the idea of
free speech if nothing else. That was
all before the quest for our version
of Ingsocian Newspeak.

Welcome. You have entered the
stanza of thus: hate—you cannot
regulate something that is
impossible to define the details of,
that opportunists will attempt to
define anyway, thus you can no
longer talk about contentious issues

because they might offend, thus you
stop thought, thus you stop the
ability to solve world problems.
        You have to be able to offend in
order to speak because someone
somewhere will take offence to
something you say.
        You ban it publicly, you push it
to the underhand underground
where the seedy abortionist lives,
where malice in the laboratory takes
root, fracturing the vines of
harmony we tread on. Let the racist
have his platform. Let him be
exposed for his idiotic ramblings,
judging others based on how they
are born, a different shade of the
same flower.
        A right to free speech amid an
outflow of painlessness—the second
you are born, there are not any rules
over what you can and cannot say.
Writing oneself onto life's script is a
basic human right. The second you
start 'you can say this but you can't
say that,' you become opportunity
hanging from a picture hook. Oh
Miss, he said, she said. The
playground politicians start slurring
like the over-drugged.
        Leader of the opposition: there
should be free speech but there are
certain rules where you cannot say
this, that and what have you. Wait, I
have just thought of something else

As they start thrashing out the above argument, see how uncomfortable it makes them, and the more so, the more items they add to the 'you can't say that' column. The reason for that uncomfortableness? They don't want to offend anyone, least of all themselves.

The degeneracy of the witch hunter—frying people's reputations 'cause they might have said one thing out of place. Hunters may go unseen but others do not wish them to be seen. Start your smear campaign against forgiveness beggars. One liver down in the vodka night.

Find something else to do like measuring emptiness more by what you do not have than what you do. Watch the lips move the words you in your composed mind unhinge from.

Maybe this argument is single-sided. I will see this in a different shade when not gathering light in my arms, only to find it obscured by them.

This is just my sentiment this mile on the path, and if you do not agree with the general gist, then you have the freedom not to.

Debauchery Diaries

Must you insist on the Prosecco again?
The smoke blows a kiss, killing me instantly
killing any goodness I ever had left
rising to yet another ceiling,
the ceiling of hers, to mine, not better nor worse, like anyone's to
smoke.
Her mind is full of men not me
I mind, a little
— jealousy was always a strong point of mind; mine, mind.
Enough about me, enough about this jealous fool, his ill-formed
marrow, his Judas kiss
— what of her?
She is a rare woman on dissimilar tracks
from the train I will take of the morn,

all aboard, say she will,
a friend lost
in spirit afresh.

Christmas List

I'm going back to the city
where the lights never change
emitting messages that glare.

After I realised I would not go back, I learned that:

☑ I am more of a people pleaser than I thought I let go of

Before I realised I would not go back, I learned that:

☑ When your parent finds someone new, not only is it getting used to the new person in their relationship, it is getting used to how they both are with each other, and then how the parent has become someone new

Less important lessons I learned were:

☑ Being assertive is like taking out the recycling
☑ Good friends ask the right questions
☑ People pleasers find awesome, innovative new ways to deplete their energy tanks
☑ Poems make me feel better like weapons for the army with God on their side.

A Night Off Course

Bird is afraid
But grass is not.

Meandering breeze
Echoes in the soil
Clenches at the root
But shred, grass does not.

I'm not really here
I'm just a phony
Looking from afar
In the blissful night,
Trying for a moment

Like normality by day
When the heavens do not sing
Where hell sits uncharted

Unlike the night of course
Yelping as she sleeps.

Finding Home

Stop-start tadpoles on the windowsill
as the train does what it should.
I am en route to rejection.
With a natural airbrush for the people
the sky is cleaning itself of mist.
Troubling as it weighs in
on the countermarch home
the rain still regurgitates
its hard-boiled song.
This tadpole finds an eye,
that one its like.
With jealousies left unsandbagged
in the gusty, teary outside
walkers between blocks
of manmade warmth make
furtive plans on what's to be
done and who's to blame.
With ornithological ignorance I do
a double take on seeing around
thirty nests
in a tree thirsting from winter
yet next to no nests
in those nearby. I mostly remember it
away from inside my own body
and yet I am going
into myself. Hoping for interception
as I pass on animal flesh to Captain Birdseye
wildlife find holes in a heartbroken sky.

Is

the cat from summer's moult
pawing at the cord, gradually, not yet, now
fully blackout-blind from the nonessential sphere
in a colour-blind prism of phantasmagoria?

Irish Sea / on a bench

1.

Sealorn, bone dry
I never went to her enough.
It is not like she never came in
Leaving the night in a carcass
Of shingle and stone, the sun
Showcasing her bullion
When she wanted to go out.

Stones like hair clips on the
Skull of the land, her song is
A white cane. Walks taken
In and around pattern her
Oversized getup.

Where armies of Celts
Once rallied and marched
On the lookout
For a manmade horizon and
The coppers of the Irish Sea,
           Alchemy began.

2.

I remember the bully-boy wind

adrenaline my widow.

A probable winter, the jailer,

could have been eight.

Bench soon bodiless.

What went missing inside

my outside had to show —

a watercourse

of salt and the

sea speaking

for me

beyond

the then needless rails.

    Memory becomes rage

after a re-remembering of

hope,

shrivelling.

They are together

I am

not;

of the shadow of gulls

I am.

The Victim

I was once a calm lake.
Human shoves of water
have made a change I never
waited for
like parched roots from
drought.
Victim cards are handed
in at the reception desk of life.
Card renewals are subject
to price changes.
So what do I do now?

Forget about yourself, you can
now
everything you need is on a screen.
Well, what is your part in all this?
Are you a soliloquy a twin-flame
persona will never let you be?
A voice in a slim room
where the extras hang out?
A monologue always
finding work?
Something else, perhaps.
It is your duty
to never be an echo.

Night to Afternoon

Frost
dazzles
in emerald
soprano hollers
on the skylight, streaming
glistening organic blankets
arching everything unclean
tipping with white
going quiet again at
the move of a head. Cannot
remember it all now, just relative
delight with the man outside in a
jester's hat on a piano playing
Grieg's 'Morning Mood'
beyond the other pane

Music makes

fernstower insectsscuttlefor
visceral>cerebral
insectsscuttling anearthgrowinglegs

The Unwashed Monologue

You can relax.
This isn't another poem
about love. Nor of pursuits
for that end, nor is it about loveless
endings.

Okay
that's a lie.
Actually it is.
Should I part ways
with concealed knowledge
of the planets or a faraway star
and send them on their way
to the cochleae of sweet ears
you possess to impress
you with my secret life
as an unfledged amateur scientist,
then arouse your mind
by filling it
with scientific questions of the day?
Should I tell you
of my recent infrequent exercise
that may have slightly toned
a hidden body beneath baggy clothes?
Do you seek out truth
on your own or do you require a nudge?
How much do you really want the truth at all
if all it serves to do
is make us both worse off.

Have you been fooled by many men before
who have put up a brilliant front
in their own concealment of
behavioural nasties and hapless insecurities.
If so, did you like them anyway?
Did you like that they had lied
so desperate for your kiss?
Would you have preferred they had
told their truth
all along
getting them nowhere,
somewhere,
anywhere but here,
listening to my monologue.

There is no resolution;
no happy ending to this poem.
I just want your truth
can you help with mine?

I thought about ending the poem there,
I probably normally would,
but some force kept me on.

I don't know where this poem is going anymore.
To tell you the truth
I never really did.
I will not ask you to help with it.
Just do me this honour, if you will:
to ask to watch you in your element
would seem too clichéd (this is a poem remember,
or at any rate that is how it has dressed today.)

'I thought you said it was a monologue,' you say.

I told you I was
never much good
at this business
of telling the truth,
and you cannot interrupt me,
this is a monologue.

Instead what I ask of you
is to show me where your work finds you
or to take me on a trip to a passionate pastime
of yours
where
learning
I will watch;
help me
help me.

peace perfect peace

peace
the all-knowing silencer
or something like that
en pointe with the ways that are
    origin and place

the all-seeing captain seeing renewal
for renewal

as the lonely wait while wanting to be wanted
with suggestions ascribed to King David in Psalm 23
how free it must be to not want
    the truest happiness
peace

Imaginings of the Familial

Bandaging the bloodied sceptre
passed down like the baton from generations passed,
must you hold up those warring, quarrelling words,
watching the watering can
bathe the blade, watching the watering can
moisten roots of family trees? Rancidity of old memories hangs
cornered kindliness.

Ferment and froth,
the gallows are here

< Morphological ends borne —

Bled out the crucifix
White became red.

The harp shakes to bits by the human hand >
Where the owls tu-whit tu-whoo >
Playing like lanterns lighting the path.

Niggardly not shall money pass hands,
Through the Dales the rooks convene
So hide me like the bumblebee in a slumping cowslip
All I see is a shroud of yellow
Have I entered Custard Land?
Is Spring's last birth but stillborn?
No! No!
The amnion not cut away
The embryo pure

Eyes azure in a babe
Tenderised heaven's heart
To leave no quibble of love.

Memoranda

In fifty years hence
this old tree will be gone but forgotten
not by Earth's tomb.
You and I, the living, the inanimate
will one day too be of buried matter,
but never can a soul be cloaked by
leaves enough in all the sky.

www.ingramcontent.com/pod-product-compliance
Lightning Source LLC
LaVergne TN
LVHW041752190726
843493LV00008B/2577